Ponies

Laura Marsh

SCHOLASTIC INC.
New York Toronto London Auckland
Sydney Mexico City New Delhi Hong Kong

For Alec
—L.F.M.

ISBN 978-0-545-43362-4

12 11 10 9 8 7 6 5 4 3 2 1   13 14 15 16/0

Printed in the U.S.A.   40

First Scholastic printing, December 2011

Design by Yay Design

Photo credits: Cover, Philip Tull/ Oxford Scientific/ Photolibrary.com; 1, Makarova Viktoria/ Shutterstock; 2, Tim Graham/ The Image Bank/ Getty Images; 4, Gallo Images/ Getty Images; 6, Eric Isselée/ Shutterstock; 7 (top left), Ocean/ Corbis; 7 (top right), Image Source/ Corbis; 7 (left center), Mikhail Kondrasho iStockphoto.com; 7 (right center), Lenkadan/Shutterstock; 7 (bottom left), Eduard Kyslynskyy/ Shutterstock; 7 (bottom right), Daniel Gale/ Shutterstock; 8, Jane Burton/ naturepl.com; 9, Fionline digitale Bildagentur GmbH/ Alamy; 10-11, Cornelia Doerr/ Photographer's Choice/ Getty Images; 11, ARCO/ naturepl.com; 12 (left), Kristel Richard/ naturepl.com; 12 (right), blickwinkel/ Alamy; 13 (top left), Juniors Bildarchiv/ Alamy; 13 (top right), Rachel Faulise; 13 (bottom left), Fo Grebler/ Alamy; 13 (bottom right), Zuzule/ Shutterstock; 14 (top left), teamtime/ iStockphoto.com; 14 (top right), pastoor/ iStockphoto.com; 14 (bottom lef Andries Oberholzer/ Shutterstock; 14 (bottom right), Matti/ Alamy; 15 (top left), George Clerk/ iStockphoto.com; 15 (top right), enis izgi/ iStockphoto.com; (bottom left), Oshchepkov Dmitry/ Shutterstock; 15 (bottom right), Lagui/ Shutterstock; 16 (left), Geoff du Feu/ Photodisc/ Getty Images; 16 (right), Tim Burret NationalGeographicStock.com; 17 (top left), Frank Lukasseck/ Photographer's Choice/ Getty Images; 17 (top right), Kim Tegg/ National Geographic My Sho 17 (bottom left), Mikhail Kondrashov "fotomik"/ Alamy; 17 (bottom right), verity johnson/ iStockphoto.com; 18-19, Steve Cicero/ Corbis; 20-21, Flickr RF/ Get Images; 22, hulton archive/ Getty Images; 22 (Background), Torkile/ iStockphoto.com; 23, Jack Delano/ Hulton Archive/ Getty Images; 24-25, Westend61/ Get Images; 25 (top), Dorling Kindersley/ Getty Images; 25 (center), Dorling Kindersley/ Getty Images; 25 25 (bottom), Lynn Johnson/ NationalGeographicStock.co 26, Medford Taylor/ National Geographic/ Getty Images; 27 (top), Danny Smythe/ iStockphoto.com; 27 (right center), Borodaev/ Shutterstock; 27 (left center), J niors Bildarchiv/ Alamy; 27 (bottom), Michael Westhoff/ iStock photo.com; 27 (top left), Ben Molyneux Sports/ Alamy; 28 (top), Hugh Threlfall/ Alamy; 28 (cente Dorling Kindersley/ Getty Images; 28 (bottom left), Timothy Large/ Alamy; 28 (bottom right), Dorling Kindersley/ Getty Images; 29, Blue Destiny/ Alamy; 30 (lef Anja Hild/ iStockphoto.com; 30 (right), Iurii Konoval/ iStockphoto.com; 31 (top left), Igum nova Irina/ Shutterstock; 31 (top right), Charles Mann/ iStockphot com; 31 (bottom left), jadimages/ Shutterstock; 31 (bottom right), Sian Lewis/ iStockphoto.com; 32 (top left), Rachel Faulise; 32 (top right), Steve Cicero/ Corbis; (bottom left), Jane Burton/ naturepl.com; 32 (bottom right), Ocean/ Corbis

Table of Contents

It's a Pony!

Ponies are
special animals.
They are
beautiful and
strong. They
are kind and
loyal. They
like to be around
people and
other animals.

What Is a Pony?

A pony is a kind of horse.

Horses and ponies are measured in hands. Most pony breeds are 14.2 hands or shorter.

= equals four inches

Horse   Pony

long legs

short legs

LEGS

sleek body

wide body

BODY

tall

short

HEIGHT

A Foal Is Born!

Pony Word

MARE:
A female horse

It's springtime. A mare gives birth to a baby pony. The baby is called a foal. Welcome, little one!

A foal can stand soon after birth.
It is wobbly on its feet at first.

The foal will run and play before lon[g].

Q What did the pony say when it fell?

A I've fallen and I can't giddyup!

All ponies are called foals in the first year.

Then young female ponies are called fillies.

Young male ponies are called colts.

Pony Breeds

There are many kinds of ponies all over the world.

Some pony breeds have been around for many, many years. Others are newer breeds.

Section A Welsh Mountain Pony

Exmoor Pony

Dartmoor Pony

Assateague Pony

Connemara Pony

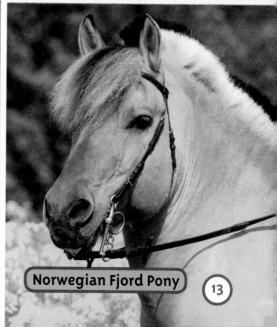

Norwegian Fjord Pony

13

Colors and Markings

palomino

spotted

blue roan

chestnut

Ponies come in lots of colors.
They can have spotted coats, too.

bright bay

skewbald

dapple grey

brown

Some ponies have white patches of hair. These are called markings.

sock

stocking

A pony's feet can have a sock or stocking.

blaze

star

A pony's head can
have a blaze, a star,
a snip, or a stripe.

snip

stripe

17

Wild Ponies

There are still wild ponies today.

A herd of wild ponies lives in Maryland and Virginia, U.S.A.

They are called the Chincoteague and Assateague ponies.

Chincoteague?
Say *SHING-keh-teeg*

Assateague?
Say *AS-seh-teeg*

Pony Word

HERD: A large group of animals that live together

Q What do you call a pony that lives next door?

A A neighhh-bor!

The herd has been around for more than 500 years!

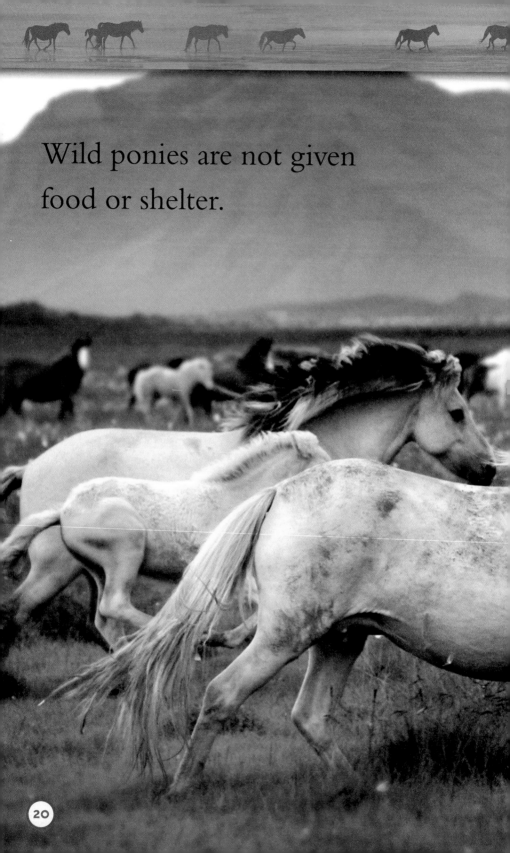

Wild ponies are not given
food or shelter.

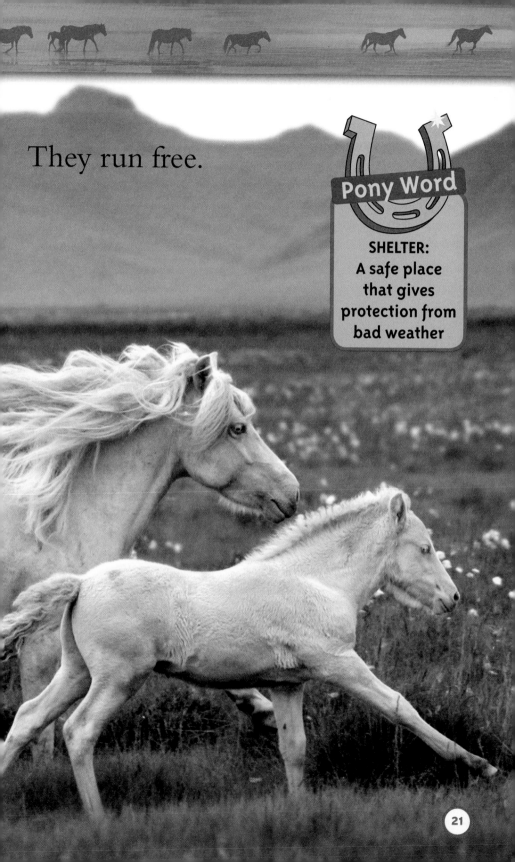

They run free.

Pony Word

SHELTER:
A safe place that gives protection from bad weather

Ponies in the Past

Ponies in the past were used for work.

Ponies pulled carriages around town. They carried people and things.

pony-drawn carriage

coal mine pony

Ponies also worked on farms, in the mountains, and in coal mines.

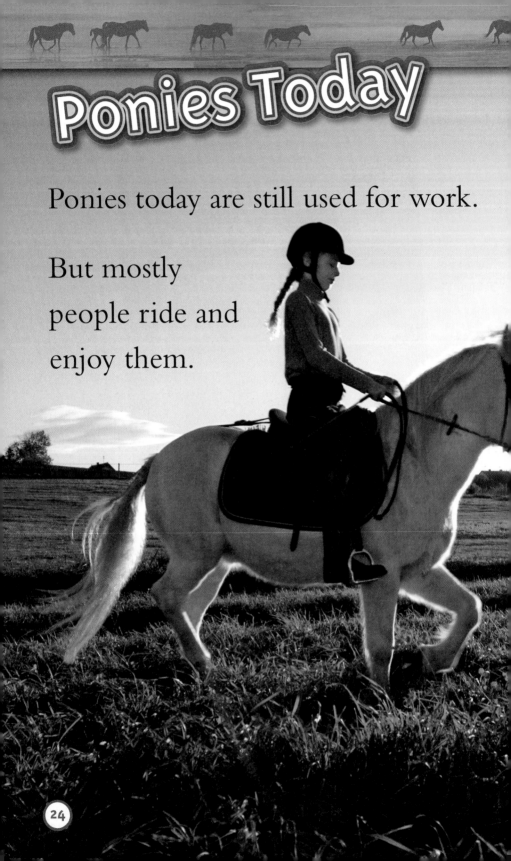

Ponies Today

Ponies today are still used for work.

But mostly people ride and enjoy them.

People ride ponies in shows and races. They ride ponies on trails.

They even ride them on vacations.

Caring for a Pony

Ponies make great pets.

But they are a lot of work!

Q What animal always goes to bed with its shoes on?

A A pony!

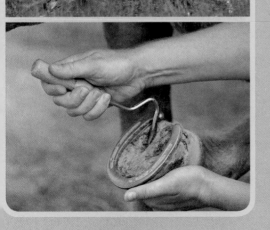

Every day
a pony needs
fresh food and
water, exercise,
brushing,
and cleaning.

27

Riding

The work is done. Now it's time to ride!

riding helmet

You will need special clothes. The clothes protect you and the pony.

riding pants called jodhpurs

Jodhpurs?
Say *JOD-purrs*

gloves

riding boots

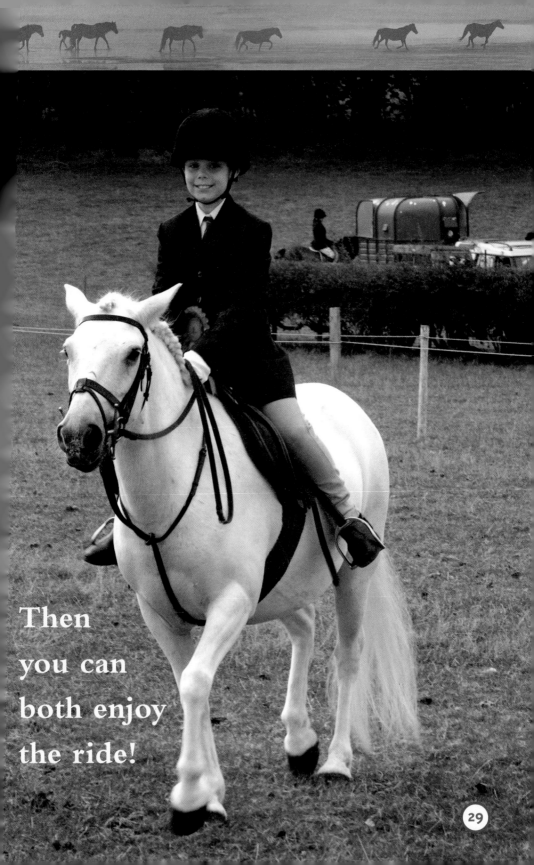

Then
you can
both enjoy
the ride!

What in the World?

These pictures show close-up views of pony things. Use the hints below to figure out what's in the pictures. Answers on page 31.

HINT: This pony marking rhymes with "gaze."

HINT: A pony rider sits here.

WORD BANK

| mane | blaze | helmet | saddle | star | foal |

3

HINT: A baby pony is called this for the first year.

4

HINT: You need to wear this when you ride.

5

HINT: A pony's neck has this long hair.

6

HINT: This pony marking rhymes with "car."

Answers: 1. blaze, 2. saddle, 3. foal, 4. helmet, 5. mane, 6. sta...

31

BREED: A group of animals that have similar features and look alike

HERD: A large group of animals that live together

MARE: A female horse

SHELTER: A safe place that gives protection from bad weather